GREAT EXPLORER
MAZES

Roger Moreau

Sterling Publishing Co., Inc.
New York

Library of Congress Cataloging-in-Publication Data

Moreau, Roger, 1935-
    The great explorer maze book / Roger Moreau.
        p.   cm.
    Includes index.
    Summary: Contains twenty-three mazes based on discoveries made by
real explorers.
    ISBN 0-8069-9606-4
    1. Explorers—Juvenile literature.   2. Maze puzzles—Juvenile
literature.   [1. Explorers.   2. Maze puzzles.   3. Puzzles.]
I. Title.
G175.M67 1997
910'.92—dc21   97-378
                                                                                      CIP
                                                                                       AC

4   6   8   10   9   7   5   3

Published by Sterling Publishing Company, Inc.
387 Park Avenue South, New York, N.Y. 10016
© 1997 by Roger Moreau
Distributed in Canada by Sterling Publishing
% Canadian Manda Group, One Atlantic Avenue, Suite 105
Toronto, Ontario, Canada M6K 3E7
Distributed in Great Britain and Europe by Cassell PLC
Wellington House, 125 Strand, London WC2R 0BB, England
Distributed in Australia by Capricorn Link (Australia) Pty Ltd.
P.O. Box 6651, Baulkham Hills, Business Centre, NSW 2153, Australia
Manufactured in the United States of America
All rights reserved

Sterling ISBN 0-8069-9606-4

Contents

A NOTE ON THE
SUGGESTED USE OF THIS BOOK

As you work your way through the mazes of this book, try not to mark them. This will enable you to take the journey over and over again and will give your friends a chance to take the journey without showing them the routes you took.

Special warning: If the journey appears too difficult, avoid the temptation to start at the end and work your way backwards. This technique would be a violation of the rules and could result in a severe reprimand.

Cover Maze: To explore this ancient Mayan Temple, you must climb the stairway. You can move up the stairway by finding a clear path around the creatures.

INTRODUCTION

The urge to explore and discover began with the very first people. These explorers probably went forth when they began to wonder what was on the other side of the hill, beyond the mountain range, or around the river bend. This urge has taken man from ocean to ocean, continent to continent, and now into space. It is a fascinating and exciting story that began long ago, goes on today, and will continue.

What is known as the Great Age of Discovery began in the 1400s, when countries in Europe desired to make money by trading with the Indies. When the Turks blocked popular Eastern trade routes after 1453, Europeans set out to find new routes. They had newer, faster, and more seaworthy ships that could hold greater loads than earlier ships, so, over the next 200 years, they sailed on the oceans, discovering and exploring new lands and finding new routes. During that time they found out more about the world than had ever been known before.

Many explorers were away from home for years. They suffered greatly and sometimes gave their lives. Their efforts required uncommon courage, strength, determination, and perseverance. They sometimes experienced the joy of victory, and too often suffered great defeat. The successful explorers had to be men of unselfish character who had complete dedication to their quests.

On the following pages you will have a chance to learn about many great explorers and follow in their footsteps. The way will not be easy. It will take courage, determination, and perseverance on your part to be successful. Even though you will face danger, sacrificing your life will, fortunately, never be required.

Now, boldly go forth . . . as they did. Good luck!

Roger Moreau

EARLY EXPLORERS

Marco Polo was an Italian explorer who explored central Asia and China between 1271 and 1292. He helped bring unknown information about the Orient back to Europe. He also made friends with the famous Mongol conqueror Kublai Khan, who gave Polo many gifts. Now, you have to reach Kublai Khan's camp **(page 7)**. Find a clear path. You can go up and down ladders and through tower openings when you travel on the Great Wall of China.

Christopher Columbus set sail from Spain on August 3, 1492, hoping to find a new route to the East by sailing west. His fleet consisted of three ships: the *Santa María*, the *Pinta*, and the *Niña*. They were sailing into unknown waters, and the three ships were greatly affected by the wind and currents. Finally, on October 12, 1492, Columbus sighted land, an island he named San Salvador. Now, *you* have to stay within the wind and current lines as you retrace Columbus's route **(pages 8 and 9)**. You must visit every island, and you cannot sail back over your own route.

The Portuguese explorer *Vasco da Gama* became the first person to sail around the Cape of Good Hope to India, in May 1498. When he returned with a cargo of spice, the king promoted him to the rank of Admiral of the Sea of India. See if you can bring back spices from India like da Gama **(page 10)**. There are many dangers. Find a clear path. If you're successful, maybe you'll also get a promotion.

Francisco Vásquez de Coronado was a Spaniard who explored the American Southwest in 1540. He was in search of the Seven Cities of Cibola and hoped to find gold. Instead, he discovered many ancient Indian dwellings, the Continental Divide, and the Grand Canyon. In this maze **(page 11)**, climb the ladders to reach the cliff dwellings.

When Coronado entered this dwelling **(pages 12 and 13)**, he was sure he'd find gold. You were probably expecting to, also. Sorry! Be careful not to disturb the tarantulas as you find a clear and fast exit to the right.

Henry Hudson was a British sea captain who hoped to find a passage to the Far East by sailing around North America. He explored the northeast coast of America and on his fourth voyage, in 1610, entered Hudson Bay. In this maze **(page 14)**, you have to try to find a way, by ship, to get to Hudson Bay. Use this map. It was drawn by one of Hudson's sailors who, unfortunately, was seasick when he drew it.

James Cook was a British mariner who made many voyages exploring and mapping the regions in the South Pacific Ocean. On his first voyage there in 1768, he sailed around Cape Horn and reached New Zealand, where he mapped the North and South Islands. Rounding Cape Horn is no simple task, as you will see **(page 15)**. The winds are harsh and the waves high. Find your way between the waves to reach the Pacific.

Great Wall of China

To reach Kublai Khan's camp, navigate a clear path on and around the Great Wall of China. You can go up and down ladders and through tower openings.

San Salvador Island

To retrace Christopher Columbus's route to San Salvador Island, make sure you stay

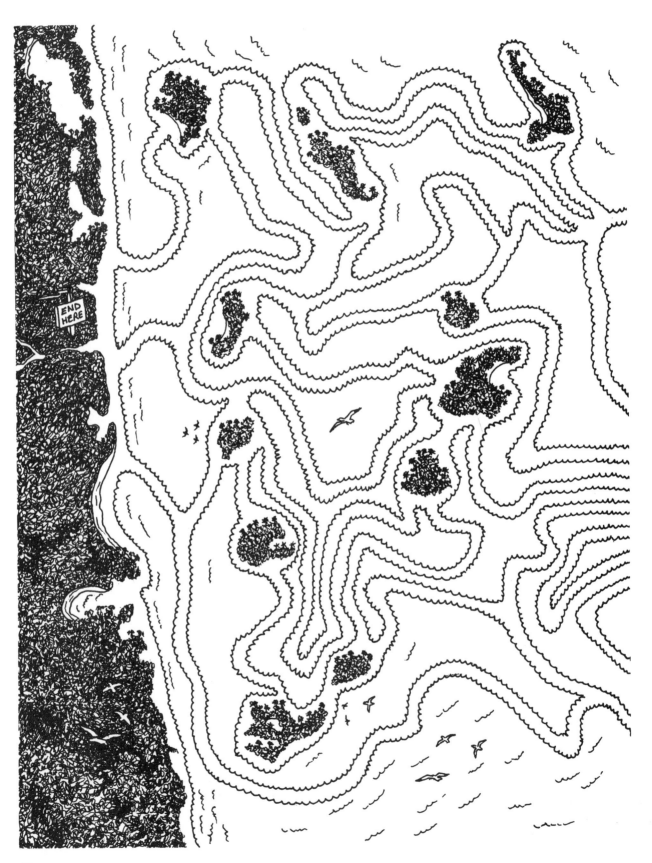

within the wind and current lines, that you visit every island, and that you do not sail back over your own route.

India Spice Shop

To reach the Spice Shop of India, you must find a clear path past the animals and other hazards and over the openings in the earth.

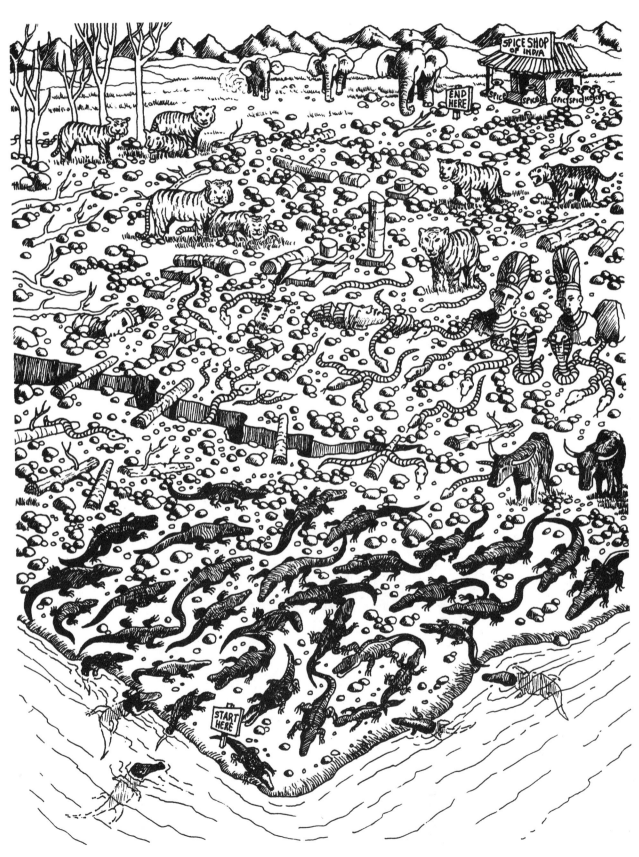

Indian Cliff Dwellings

To reach the ancient Indian cliff dwellings, climb the ladders.

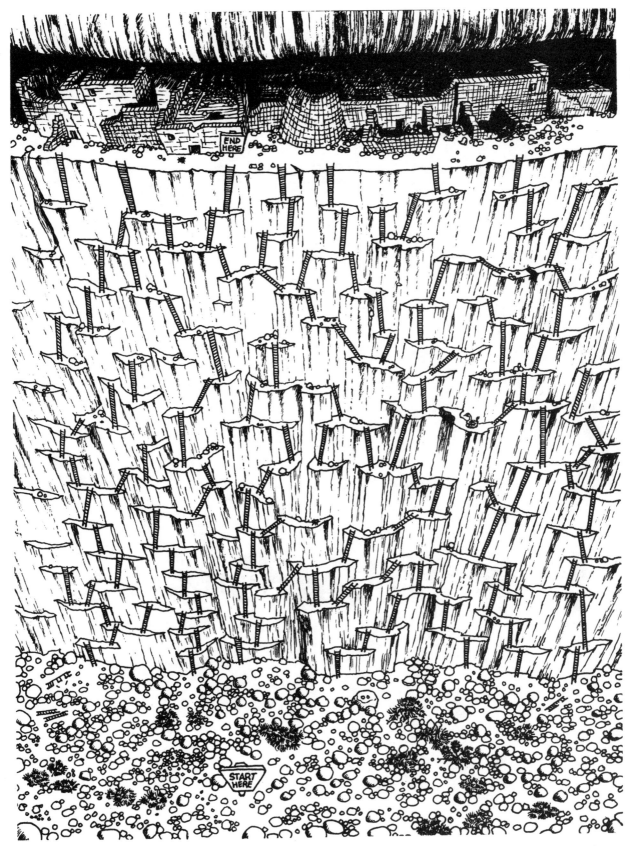

Inside an Indian Cliff Dwelling

There is no gold in this cliff dwelling, only tarantulas. To reach the exit, find a path through them.

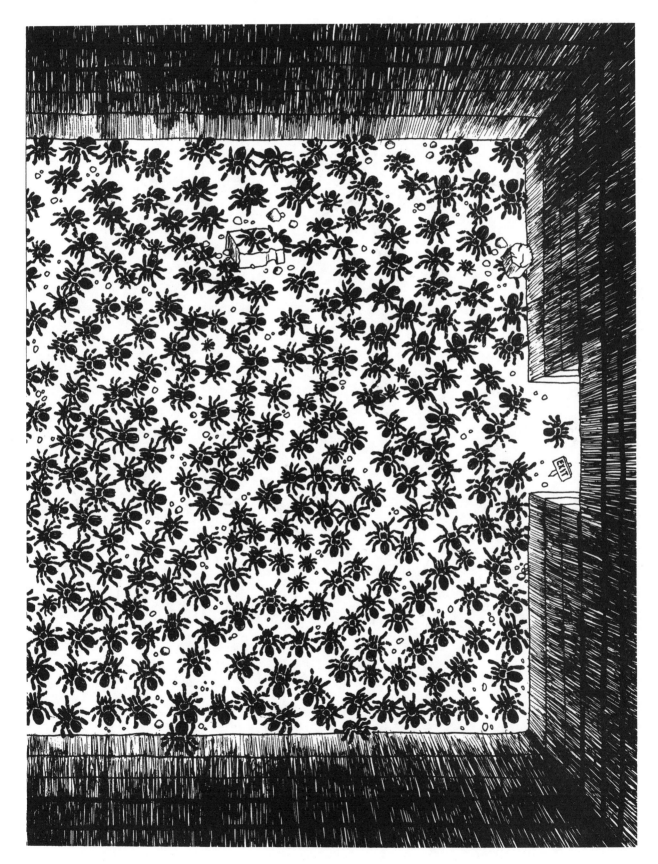

Hudson Bay

To sail to Hudson Bay, find the right tributary.

Cape Horn

To round Cape Horn and reach the Pacific Ocean, you must find your way between the waves.

19TH-CENTURY EXPLORERS

For many years, starting as early as the 1500s, explorers attempted unsuccessfully to find a Northwest Passage. *John Franklin* was a British naval explorer who made three attempts in the early 1800s. On his third expedition, in 1821, while Franklin was attempting to map the Arctic coastline, tragedy struck. An early winter set in and all of the expedition perished. In this maze **(page 17)**, you must find your way up the Hood River to Coronation Gulf, which is choked with blocks of ice. Find your way through the ice to reach Kent Peninsula. A herd of caribou is passing through the area, so avoid the places on the river where they block the way. Try to get through before winter sets in.

In May 1804, *Meriwether Lewis* and *William Clark* set out to travel up the Missouri River in an effort to find and map a way to the Pacific Ocean. Their journey took two years and covered 8,000 miles round-trip. Finding their way wasn't easy. They got help from an Indian woman named Sacagawea, who served as a guide and interpreter during their westward march in Shoshone Indian country. **On pages 18 and 19**, you must find your way up the Missouri River, and then up eastward-flowing streams to the Continental Divide—the area that extends south-southeast from northwest Canada to South America. Next, find the right trail that will enable you to discover a westward-flowing stream that will take you to the mighty Columbia River and the Pacific Ocean. You won't have Sacagawea to help you, but you will have an old Indian map.

During the mid-19th century, a great effort was made in Africa to find the headwaters of the Nile River. In 1858, two British explorers, *Richard Burton* and *John Hanning Speke*, discovered Lake Victoria and suggested that it might be the source of the White Nile. In 1866, *David Livingstone*, a Scottish medical missionary, set out to find the source of the White Nile and was not heard from for several years. In 1869, an American reporter named *Henry Stanley* set out to find Livingstone. He found him at Lake Tanganyika, which had been discovered by Burton and Speke in 1858. When he first saw Livingstone, he uttered those famous words "Dr. Livingstone, I presume?" See if you can find your way up the White Nile to Lake Victoria **(pages 20 and 21)**. You must row upstream to the falls and then hike around any falls to get into the streams above them. You can go up and down the streams, but you cannot row up any falls.

In 1860–1861, the Irishman *Robert O'Hara Burke* and his English companion *William Wills* became the first men to cross Australia from south to north. On the return trek, they died of starvation. Follow their route from Melbourne to the Gulf of Carpentaria **(pages 22 and 23)**. Find a clear path and take plenty of food and water.

Kent Peninsula

To find your way through the ice to reach Kent Peninsula, make sure you use a path that is not blocked by caribou.

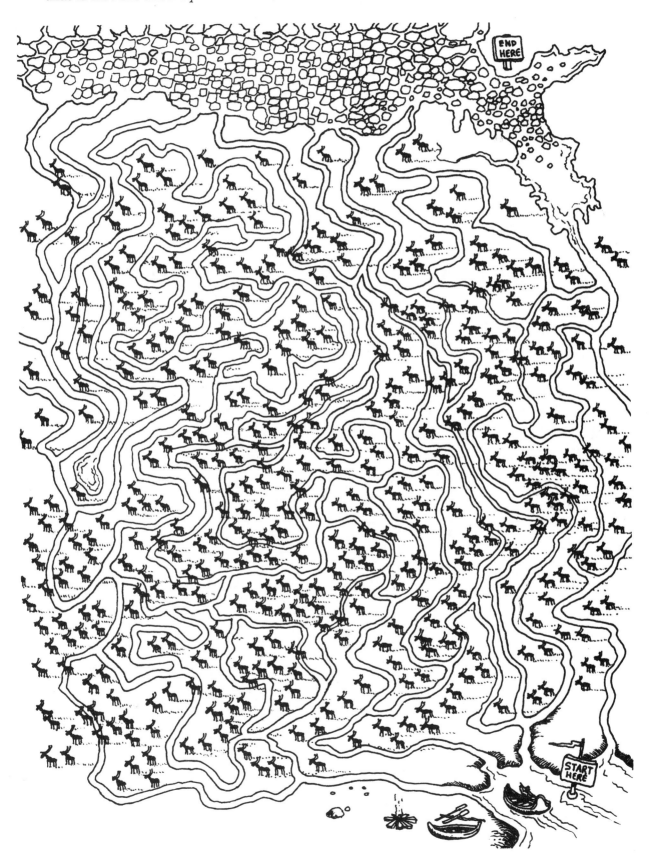

Missouri River

Your goal here is to find the correct path up the Missouri River to the Continental

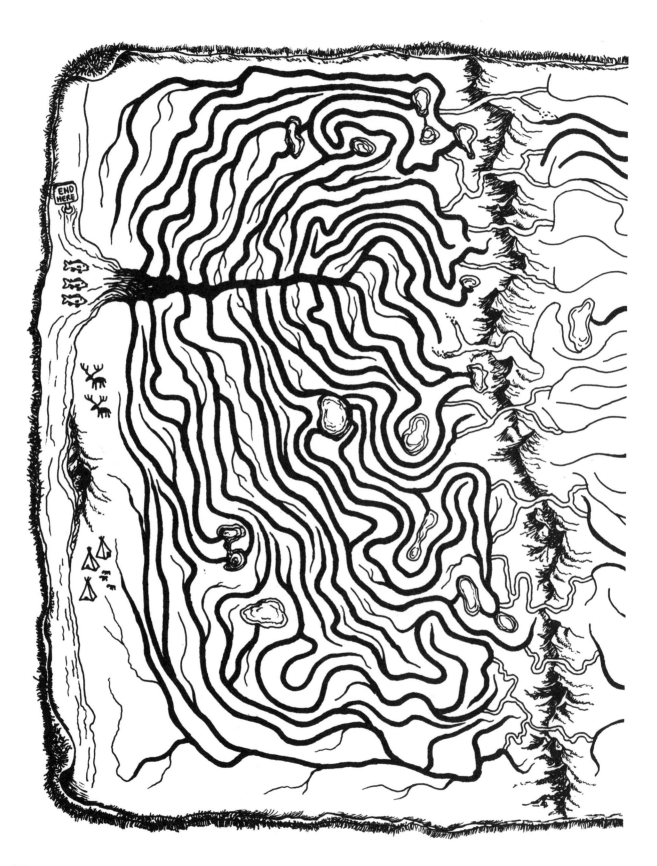

Divide, and then the trail that will take you from the Continental Divide to the Columbia River to the Pacific Ocean.

Lake Victoria

To get to Lake Victoria from the Nile River, find the correct stream to the falls, and the

END AT LAKE

correct path from the falls to the lake. Remember, you can move up and down the streams, but you cannot row up the falls.

Gulf of Carpentaria

To navigate the route from Melbourne to the Gulf of Carpentaria, find a path that avoids the wildlife and other hazards and crosses the openings in the earth.

20TH-CENTURY EXPLORERS

Commander Robert E. Peary was an American explorer who was the first man to reach the North Pole, on April 6, 1909. He trekked over drifting pack ice for 413 nautical miles. Now, you have to get to the North Pole **(page 25)**. The ice is always cracking and moving. Avoid the cracks in the pack ice and keep dry.

Now that you're there, you must return **(page 26)**—a trip of 413 nautical miles. Note that the ice has changed. Good luck!

After Peary reached the North Pole, the race was on for the South Pole. Two explorers, *Roald Amundsen* of Norway and *Robert Falcon Scott* of Great Britain, were involved in the race between 1910 and 1912. Each went by a different route. The distance to the South Pole was about 900 miles. Amundsen reached the Pole first, on December 14, 1911. He left his tent there, which Scott found when he arrived a few months later. On the return trip, Scott and his four companions froze to death. Now, you must find a path to the Pole **(page 27)**.

You made it! Now, you must get back—a trip of 900 miles **(page 28)**. Is it possible?

Hiram Bingham was an American explorer who discovered Machu Picchu, an ancient Inca city 6,270 feet high in the Andes, in 1911. Follow his map to the ancient city **(page 29)**. You can go under and on the overpasses.

Now, climb the steep trail to the city **(page 30)**. It could be tough.

Howard Carter was an English archaeologist who discovered the undisturbed tomb of the pharaoh Tutankhamen in 1922. The opening was a stairway found under tons of rocks in the Valley of the Kings in Egypt. Find a clear path to the stairway **(page 31)**.

Now, explore the tomb and find King Tut **(pages 32 and 33)**. Avoid the debris and snakes.

On July 20–21, 1969, the crew of Apollo 11—*Neil Armstrong, Edwin Aldrin, Jr.*, and *Michael Collins*—broadcast to earth from the moon, "Houston, Tranquillity Base here. The 'Eagle' has landed." Then, as Neil Armstrong stepped from the lunar module footpad onto the moon, he announced, "That's one small step for a man, one giant leap for mankind." Man had finally set foot on the moon. Now, you have a chance to explore Tranquillity Base **(pages 34 and 35)**. Do not step on or over any rocks or into any shadows.

In April 1912, the luxury ship *Titanic* struck an iceberg in the North Atlantic and went down with a loss of 1,522 people. On September 1, 1985, Robert Ballard found the *Titanic* 13,000 feet down on the ocean floor. See if you can find it in the maze **(page 36)**. A grid has been placed over the search area. Move through the openings to try to find the *Titanic*.

Explore the *Titanic* **(page 37)**. Find a clear path over the top surface of the ship.

In France, caves have been found with beautiful ancient paintings covering the walls. Now, you can discover one **(pages 38 and 39)**. This is your chance to be included with the great explorers of the past. If you are successful at exploring your discovery, name the cave after yourself. But, remember, once you go in you have to be able to get out.

North Pole

To follow in the footsteps of Commander Robert Peary and reach the North Pole, find the correct path that avoids the cracks in the ice.

North Pole

Now that you've reached the North Pole, you must find your way back.

South Pole

Now, try your luck at finding the South Pole. Once again, avoid the cracks in the ice.

South Pole

Now that you have reached the South Pole, you must find your way back.

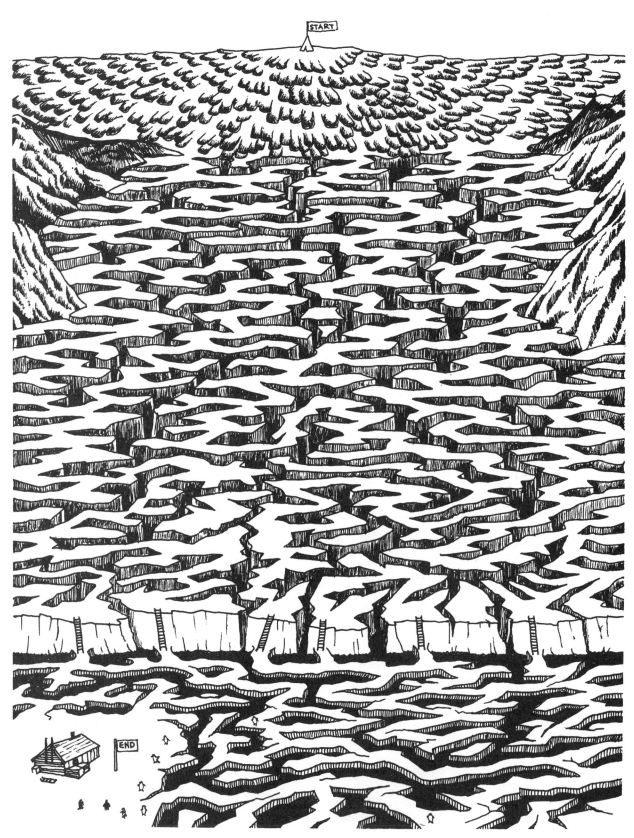

Machu Picchu

To travel to the ancient Inca city of Machu Picchu, you have to go under and on the overpasses.

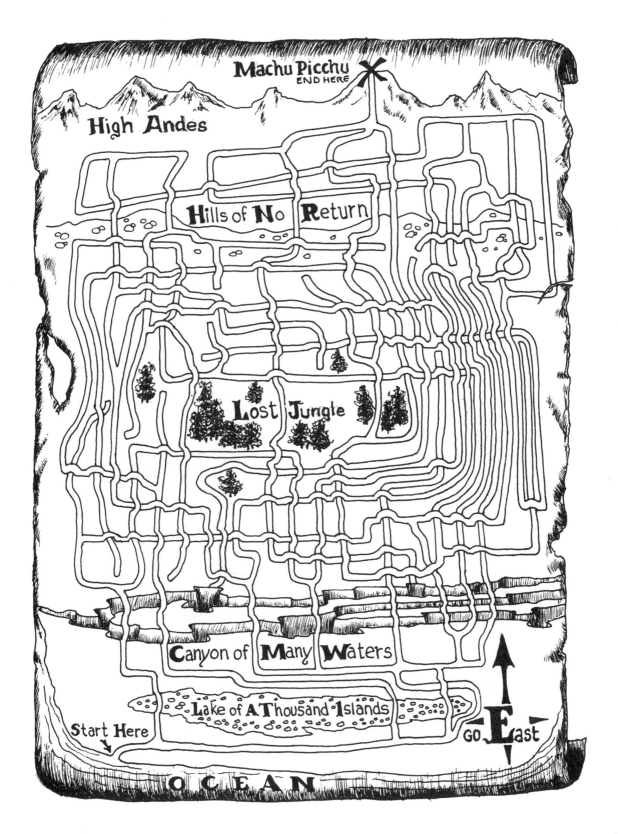

Machu Picchu

Now, climb the steep trail to the city.

START HERE

END

Tomb of Tutankhamen

Find a path to the stairway that leads to the tomb of Tutankhamen.

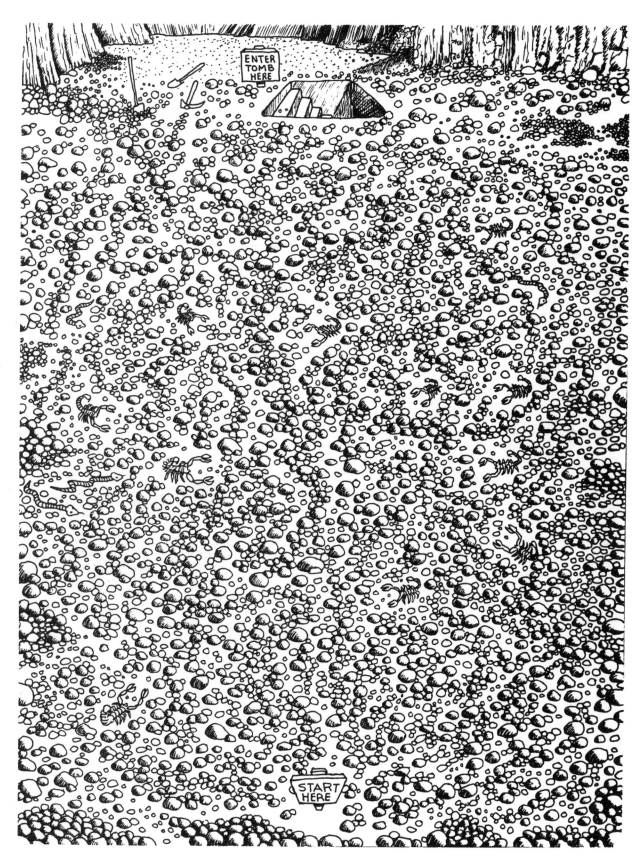

Tomb of Tutankhamen

Now that you're inside the tomb, find a path past the debris and snakes to find King Tut.

Tranquillity Base

Now that you've landed on the Moon, find a path around Tranquillity Base. Do not step on or over any rocks or into any shadows.

Titanic

To reach the *Titanic*, maneuver through the openings in the maze.

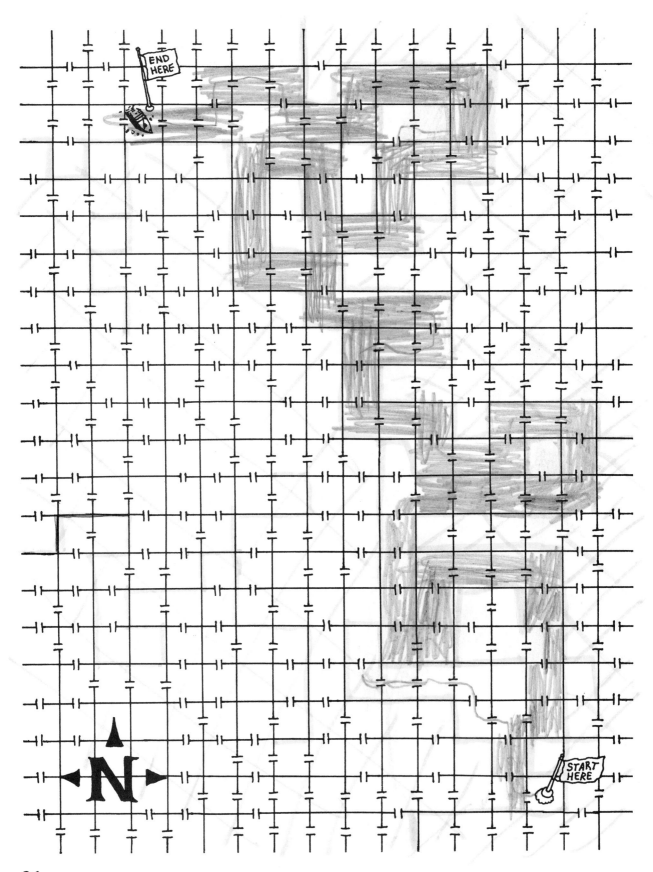

Titanic

Now that you've found the *Titanic,* explore it by traveling along a path on the top surface of the ship.

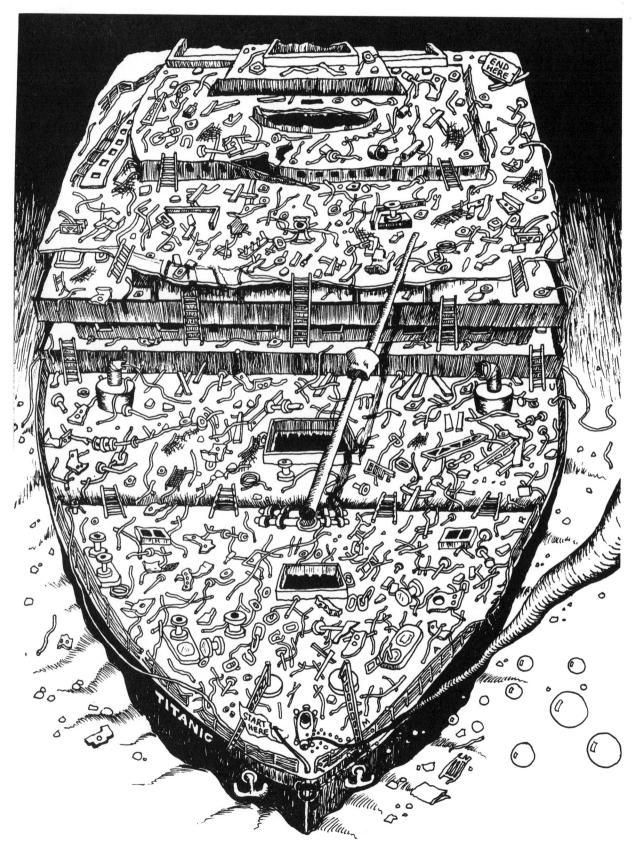

French Cave

Chart a path through this cave in the hopes of discovering ancient paintings.

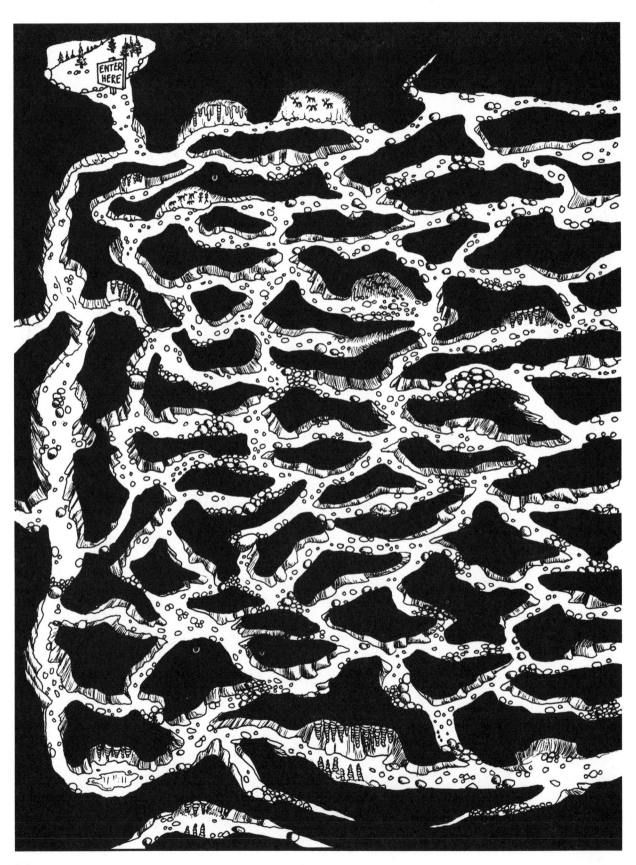

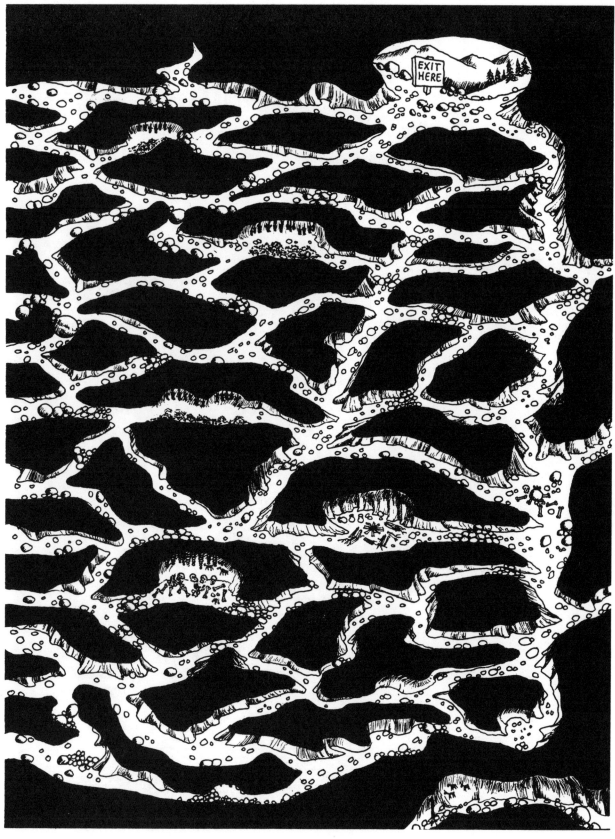

CONGRATULATIONS!

You have been successful in following in the footsteps of many of the great explorers of the past, and have learned how important it is not to get discouraged or give up. There is an exciting world out there for you to explore. Now, go forth with all the courage and determination of those past explorers and make your mark in whatever you choose to do. Remember, strive to know what is over the hill, beyond the mountain range, and around the bend in the river.

EXPLORER'S GUIDES

If you had any trouble finding your way through the mazes in this book, use the explorer's guides on the following pages. These guides should be used only in case of an emergency. The guide shown below is for the cover maze.

Great Wall of China

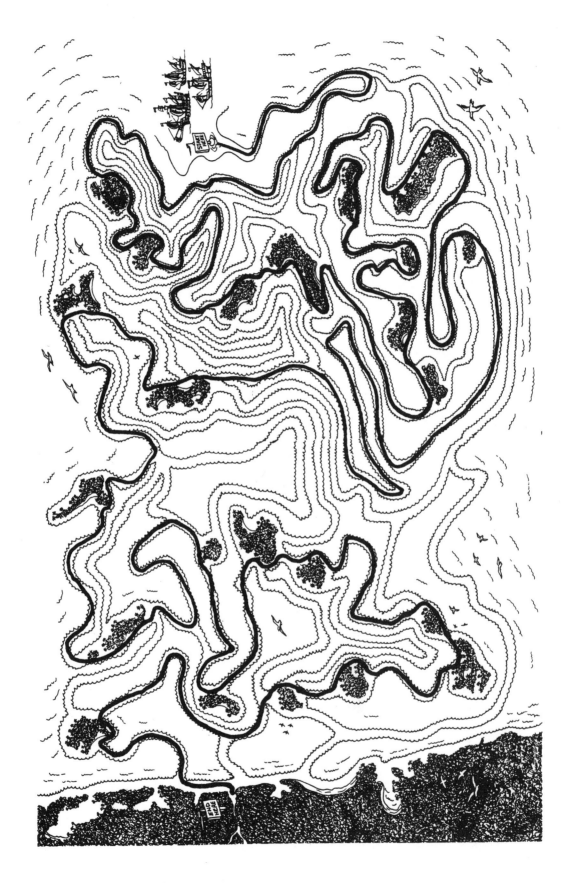

San Salvador Island

India Spice Shop

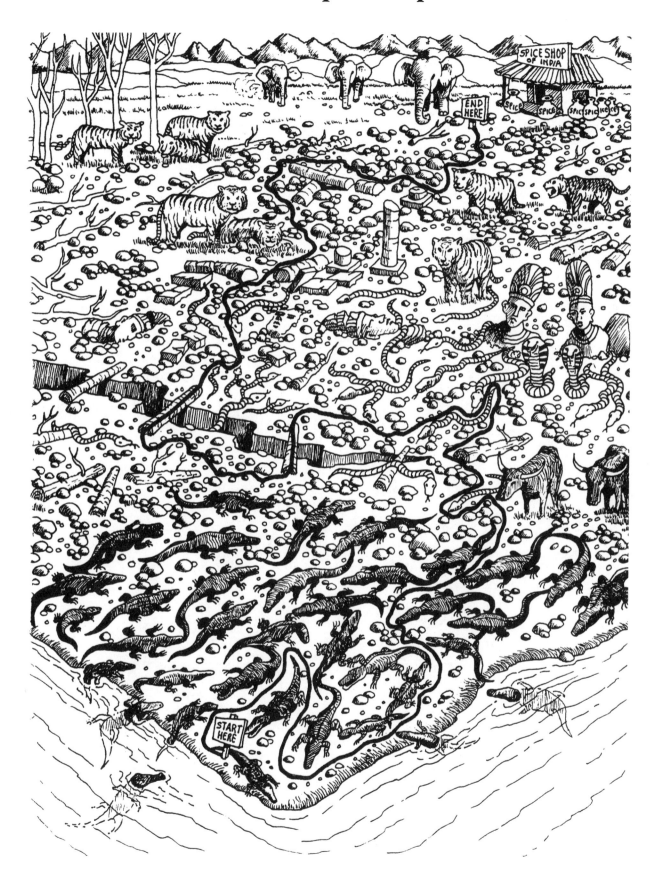

Indian Cliff Dwellings

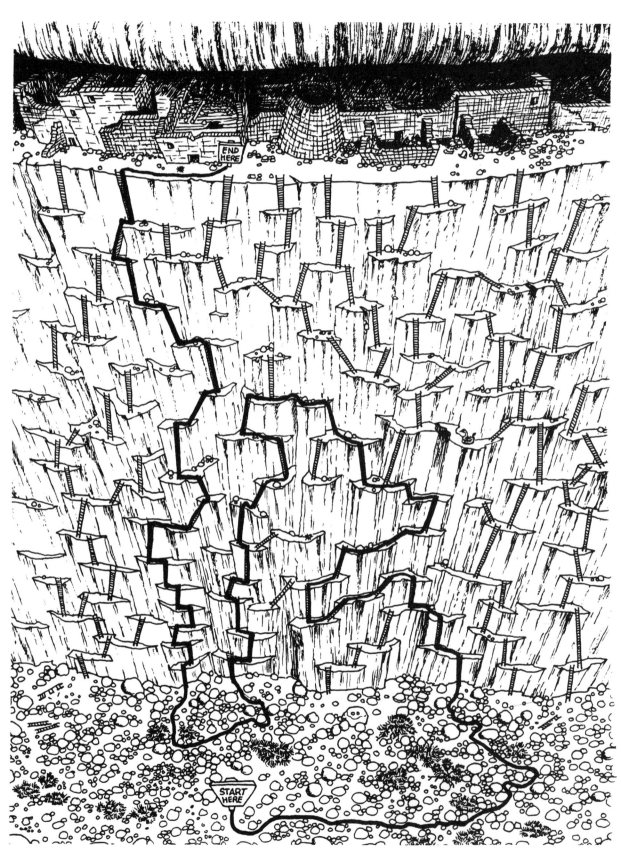

Inside an Indian Cliff Dwelling

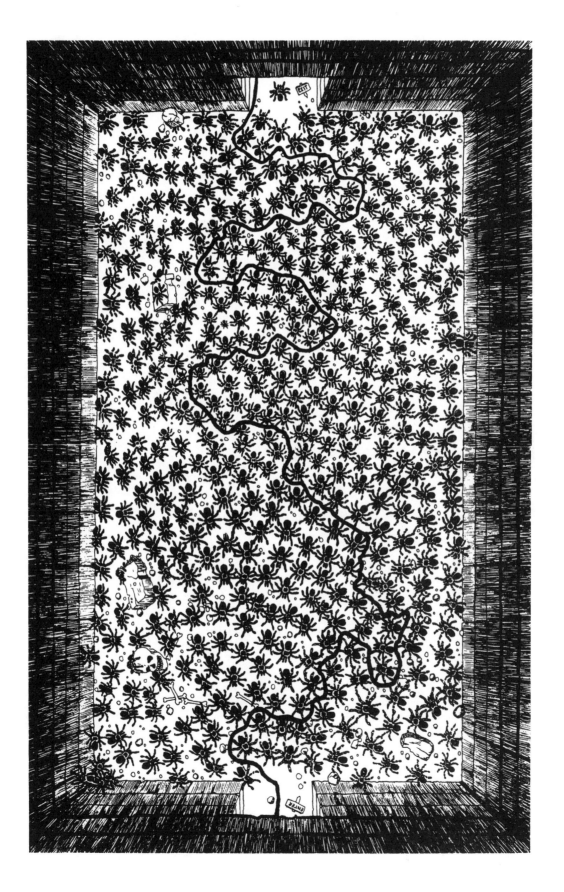

Hudson Bay

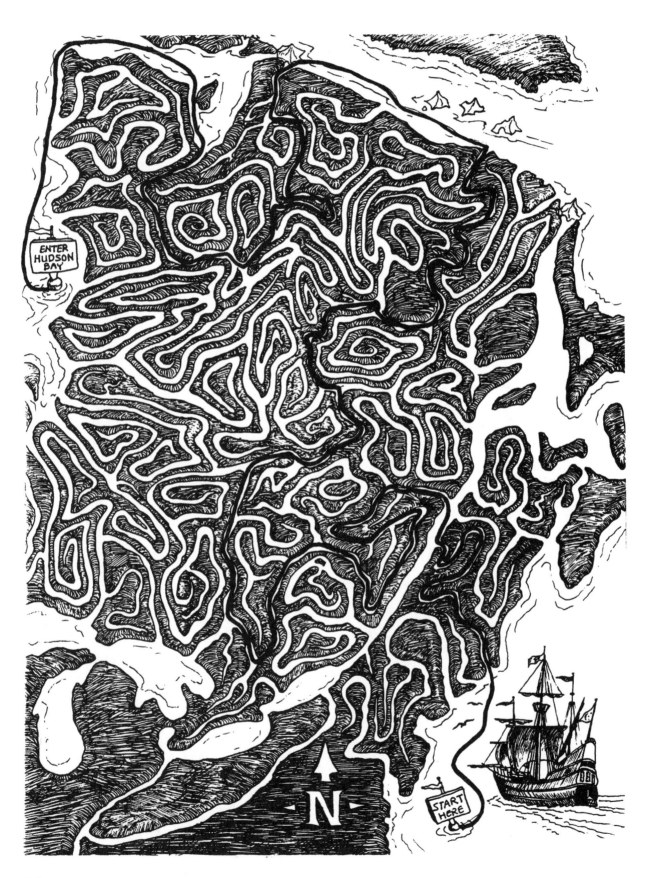

Cape Horn

Kent Peninsula

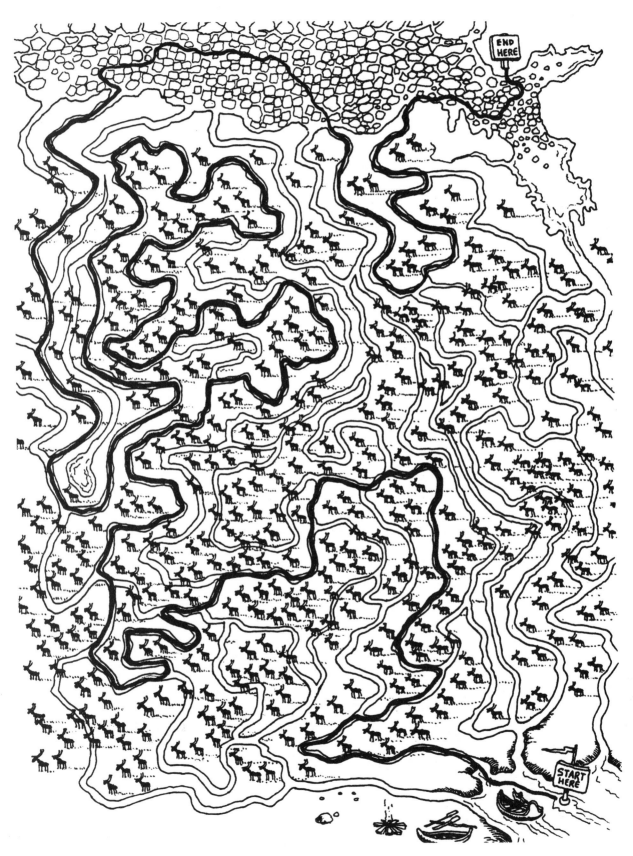

Missouri River

Lake Victoria

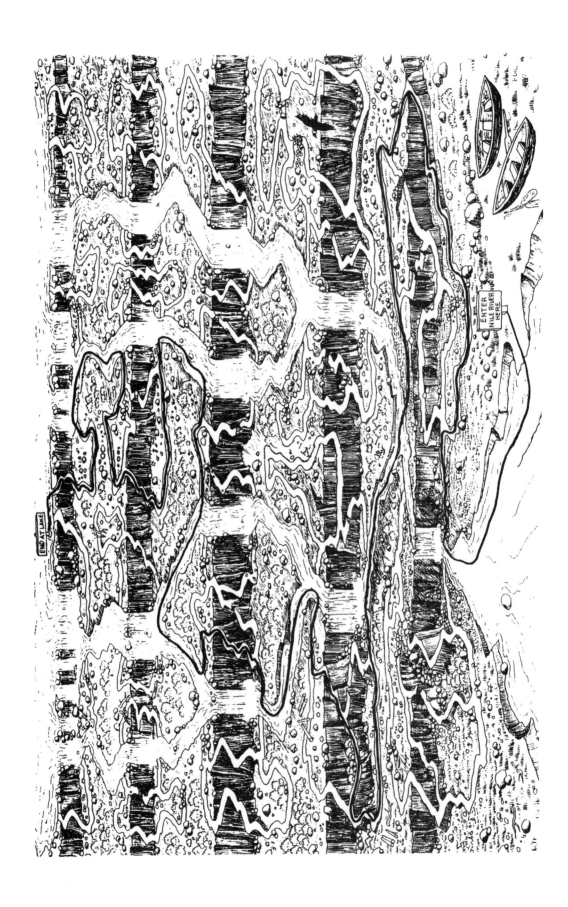

Gulf of Carpentaria

North Pole

North Pole

South Pole

South Pole

Machu Picchu

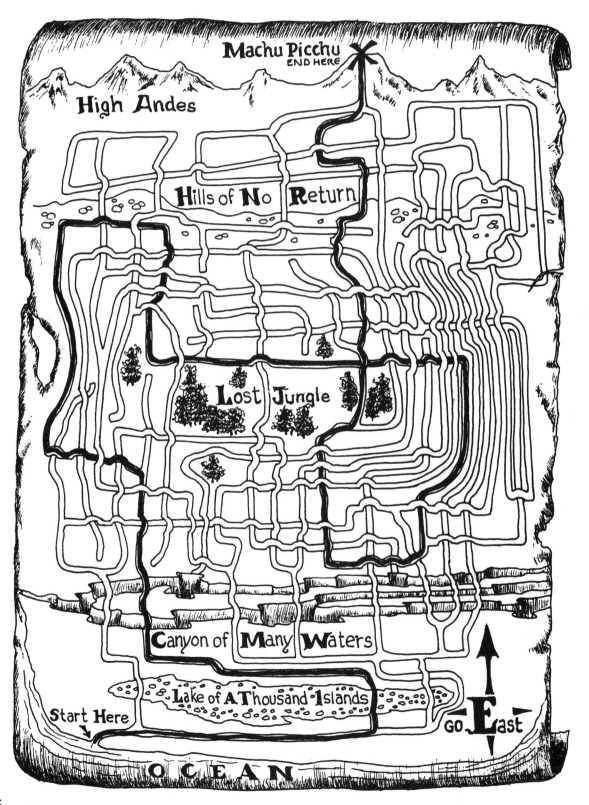

Machu Picchu

Tomb of Tutankhamen

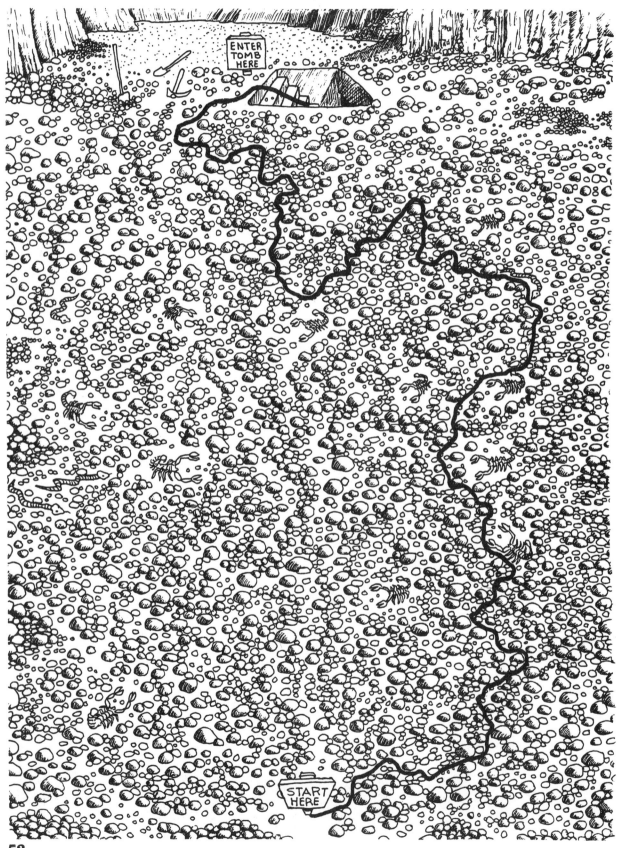

Tomb of Tutankhamen

Tranquility Base

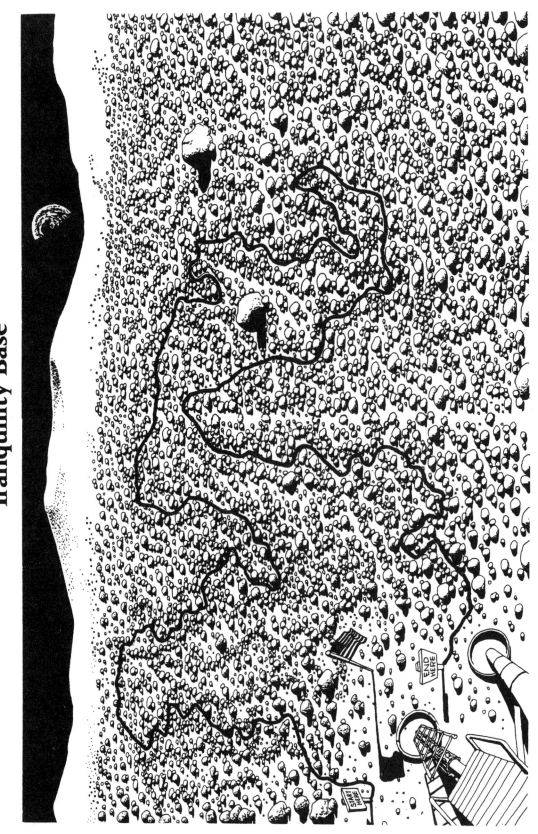

Titanic

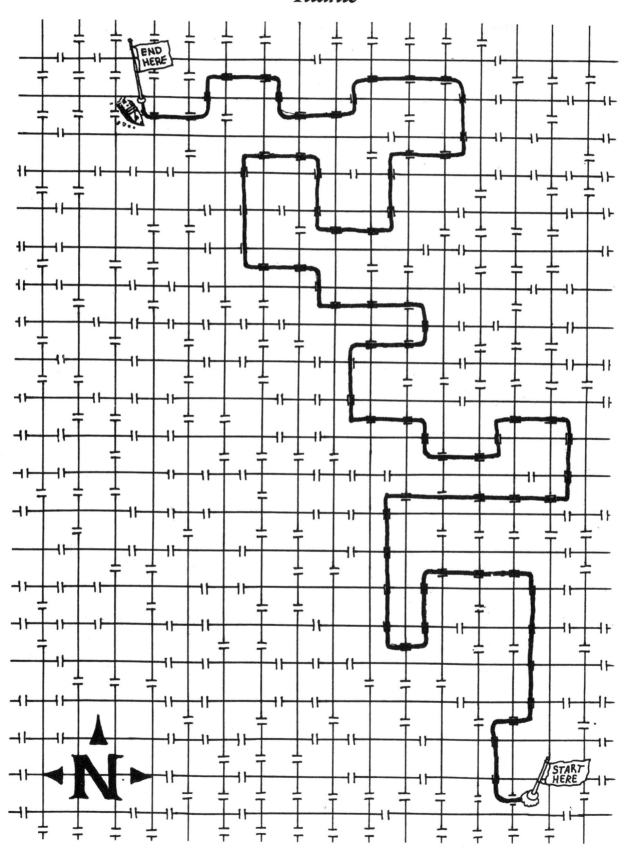

Titanic

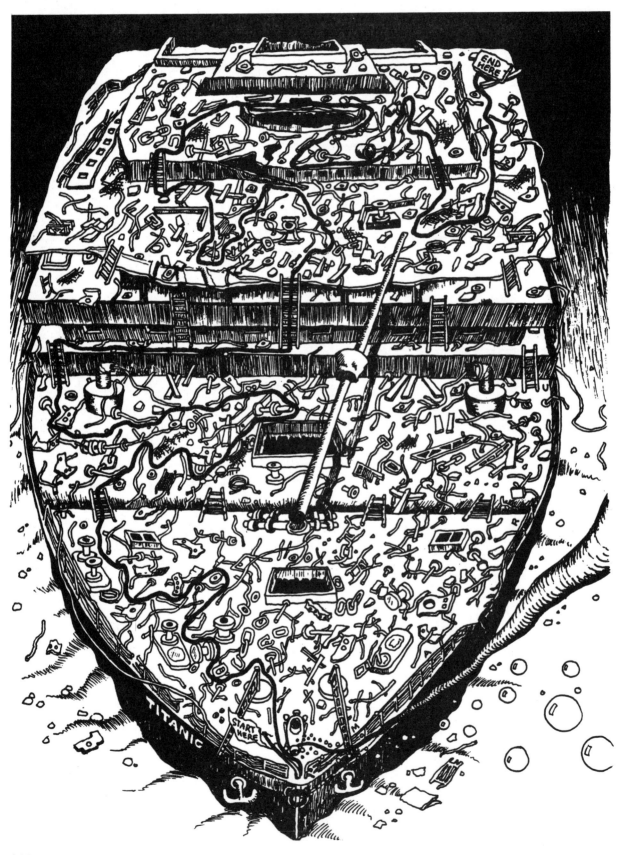

French Cave

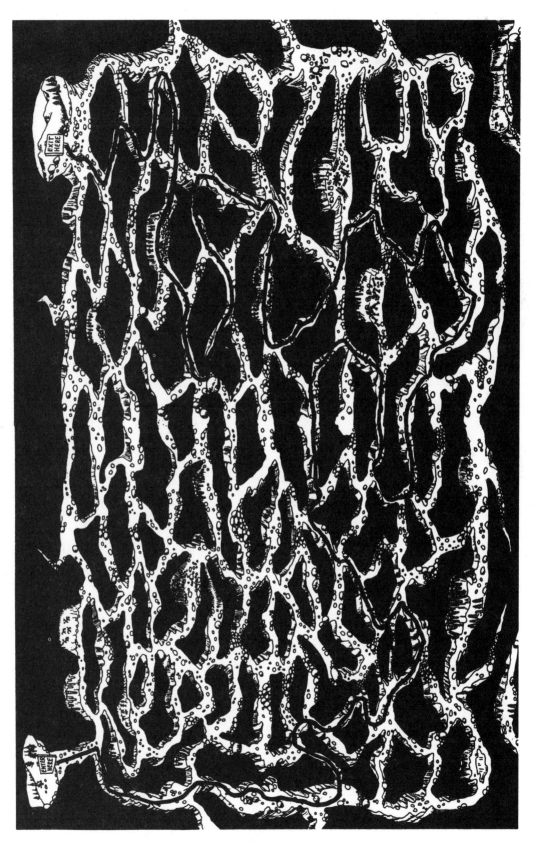

Index

Numbers in **bold** refer to puzzles, in *italics* to solutions.